The Way We Pray

———

An Introduction to
The Book of Common Prayer

———

Leonel L. Mitchell

Revised Edition

©1984, ©1997, Forward Movement Publications
412 Sycamore Street, Cincinnati, Ohio 45202-4195.
ISBN 0-88028-185-5

About the Author

The Rev. Canon Leonel L. Mitchell, Th.D.,
is Retired Professor of Liturgics
at Seabury-Western Theological Seminary.

Introduction

To both the casual inquirer and the dedicated church-goer, the liturgical worship in The Book of Common Prayer is the most obviously distinctive thing about the Episcopal Church. The liturgy not only provides structure for the public worship, it is the chief reflection of our theology and it forms the basis of our private prayers. These pages are an attempt to introduce the prayer book as the primary source for teaching Episcopalians and others about the Episcopal Church.

This material was originally prepared as part of a program for Christian Education Leadership Certification sponsored by the Episcopal Theological Seminary in Kentucky. It is intended for Christian educators and other interested persons who wish to use the Prayer Book as a resource for learning more about the Episcopal Church.

Contents

1
The Prayer Book and Liturgical Worship

What is liturgy?

The word *liturgy* means a public service. Like *service* itself it signifies a variety of things. It is literally the work of the people. Its original meaning was a public work, something someone did for someone else like repairing the roads, but it has also come to mean an occasion of public worship. Since the eucharist is the chief such act, the word *liturgy* is sometimes used simply to mean the eucharist. The Eastern Church regularly speaks of The Liturgy, or The Divine Liturgy, much as Lutherans speak of The Service.

When we use the word *liturgy* in the Episcopal Church we generally mean all of the services of The Book of Common Prayer, which is the liturgy of the Episcopal Church. In this way we may speak of the Anglican liturgy, as opposed to the Roman liturgy or the Lutheran liturgy.

The place of liturgy in the Christian life

But liturgy means more than a book. It is the way we worship God. We speak of the central place the liturgy occupies in our lives, meaning the central place which the public worship of God, and especially the eucharist, has in the lives of practicing Christians. Indeed when we speak of *practicing* Christians we usually mean those who participate in the liturgy.

This is not a modern idea. When the Emperor Diocletian sought to stamp out Christianity he forbade Christians to assemble for worship. He realized that their common assembly was at the very heart of what they were doing, and if he could stop that he could wipe out Christianity. He failed (although the automobile and professional football have had considerably more success).

Christianity is not a religion to be practiced by individuals in their solitariness. It is a way of living as a new people that involves relationships among other Christians. The weekly assembly of the Lord's people on the Lord's day to celebrate the Lord's service has always been at its center. It is not that worship is a substitute for life, but rather that it is the core and focal point of a common life. It is the eucharist which, as you will see in the final chapter, constitutes us as the people of God and our weekly assembly renews and reconstitutes us week by week. All of our concerns as a people and as individuals are brought to the assembled church and offered up to God through Jesus Christ in the Spirit-filled fellowship of the church. And from God, through Christ, in the Spirit-filled church, we receive the power and strength to be the people of God.

The church is first and foremost a worshiping community. It is the *synaxis,* the gathering together of the people of God for corporate worship, which is the heart and soul of the church's life. We say this in a great many ways. The Second Vatican Council said,

"It is through the liturgy that the faithful are enabled to express in their lives and manifest to others the mystery of Christ and the real nature of the true Church." (*Constitution on the Sacred Liturgy 2*)

In the Episcopal Church, Associated Parishes said it this way:

"Jesus Christ is the Lord of all creation and is the Head of the human race. Through Him, in the unity of the Holy Spirit, the Christian Church is called to worship God the Father, to await His kingdom, and to serve in His world . . . the Holy Eucharist is the characteristic and representative action of the Church in the fulfillment of this vocation . . . From the altar, God's redeeming and renewing power reaches out into every phase of life; to the altar every aspect of our existence is to be gathered up and offered to God through Christ in the fellowship of His Holy Spirit." (Associated Parishes, *A Parish Program 1964*)

We should not be surprised then to find the prayer book sounding this same note in its first pages, in the section entitled "Concerning the Service of the Church" (BCP 13):

"The Holy Eucharist, the principal act of Christian worship on the Lord's Day and other major Feasts, and Daily Morning and Evening Prayer, as set forth in this Book, are the regular services appointed for public worship in this Church."

We might follow this with the statements of the catechism, "An Outline of the Faith":

"The Eucharist, the Church's sacrifice of praise and thanksgiving, is the way by which the sacrifice of Christ is made present, and in which he unites us to his one offering of himself . . . The benefits we receive are the forgiveness of our sins, the

11

strengthening of our union with Christ and one another, and the foretaste of the heavenly banquet
which is our nourishment in eternal life." (BCP 859f)

The prayer book lays out at its beginning the traditional
Christian and catholic format of the life of the Church. At
its center is the Lord's service, the Holy Eucharist, celebrated by the Lord's people on the Lord's day, Sunday. It
is our common gathering as the family of God, united with
one another in Christ our head to celebrate his death and
resurrection until his coming again. But the Sunday
eucharist does not stand in isolation. Daily Morning and
Evening Prayer provide the supporting framework of corporate and personal prayer for the Sunday liturgy.

This is the on-going structure of the liturgical life of
the Church which is the focus of the new life in Christ. It
does not sit alone and isolated from the day-to-day business
of living, but permeates it and offers it all, joys, sorrows,
successes, failures, frustrations, anger, and love to God.

The Prayer Book as our liturgical book

While it is certainly true that most if not all Christians
have a liturgical book, The Book of Common Prayer
occupies a unique position, not only for us as Episcopalians but among the liturgical books of English-speaking
Christians. It has throughout the centuries exercised a for-
mative influence on all who pray in English. The early
Anglican prayer book and the King James Bible formed
English as a liturgical language and a language of prayer.
When, in the last twenty years, a contemporary form of
liturgical English has emerged, we find the prayer book
setting a standard for us still. When we compose our own

prayers they may tend to sound like the prayers of the prayer book because this is the way we have become accustomed to thinking that prayer sounds. This tends to be true whether we are composing prayers for formal use in a service or praying privately in our own words. The words and prayer forms of The Book of Common Prayer resound in our consciousness.

It is not only in language but in structure of worship that the prayer book has been a guide. It has formed the way in which we think services ought to be organized and conducted. The format of the Eucharist and Morning Prayer shape the service of many non-Episcopal churches as well.

When the prayer book made its first appearance in 1549 it replaced a collection of medieval service books. Not only did it translate the services of the Church into English but it included them all in a single printed book which could be placed in the hands of the congregation. Liturgical worship ceased to be a priestly preserve and became the concern of the entire congregation. This did not happen all at once, but it *did* happen so that today we take for granted that the words, the script for the liturgical action, will be in the hands of the entire congregation.

In the prayer book we have a complete script for the services in which we participate and consequently for the central activity of the Church and the core of our life in Christ. The book is not intended as a strait-jacket to confine the prayers of the congregation—although some have certainly treated it as though it were—but as a tool for our common celebration. Adaptation of the prayer book services to local custom and special occasions has been made easier by modern methods of duplication. The liturgical scholar James White observed recently that Gutenberg made it possible to put prayer books in the hands of the congregation, while A.B. Dick and Xerox have made such books obsolete.

When I sing in the shower I may sing any tune, in any key, at any tempo I choose. On the other hand, if I wish to sing in a chorus there are certain requirements. We need an agreement as to what we are singing, who will sing what parts, what key we shall sing it in, and at what tempo. Usually we need a leader to organize and coordinate our efforts. The same is true of worship. The prayer book provides the structure for our common prayer.

"The way we pray establishes the way we believe"

For us Episcopalians, however, The Book of Common Prayer is more than a guide to the conduct of services. It is the basic source book of our theology. This is why we resist so strongly tinkering with the prayer book. It is not that we care deeply whether the Nicene Creed comes before or after the sermon, but we care immensely about the approach to God which we find in The Book of Common Prayer and any change in it seems to portend a change in the way we approach God.

Traditionally this dependence of theology upon worship has been expressed in the Latin maxim *lex orandi lex credendi,* the way we pray establishes the way we believe. Anthropologists say much the same thing in the statement, "creed follows cult." Worship—religious activity in all its aspects, what we do and how we do it, what we say and how we say it—underlies religious belief.

These principles are, of course, equally true for all

religions, in the broadest possible sense, but most religions (certainly most Christian churches) tend to think of their worship as an action or experience in which they participate, rather than as a book. In this they are certainly correct. Episcopalians really believe this too, but we tend to express our beliefs in terms of the prayer book. Ceremonial changes, for example, which were mentioned in neither the 1928 nor 1979 prayer book, were frequently cited by churchgoers as objections to the revised prayer book. And yet it is not really the book, but the total experience of its services that is central to our theology and religion.

In a real sense, Episcopalians are liturgical theologians. We read our theology out of The Book of Common Prayer where we also find the manner in which we celebrate its services. It you want to know what the Episcopal Church believes about the birth of Jesus Christ, for example, we tend not to quote dogmatic definitions such as the one found in Article II of the 39 Articles. (BCP 868) We are more likely to quote the familiar words of the Christmas collect:

"Almighty God, you have given your only-begotten Son to take our nature upon him, and to be born of a pure virgin . . ." (BCP 213)

or the words of the Christmas Proper Preface,

"Because you gave Jesus Christ, your only Son, to be born for us; who by the mighty power of the Holy Spirit, was made perfect Man of the flesh of the Virgin Mary his mother; so that we might be delivered from the bondage of sin, and receive power to become your children." (BCP 378)

The words of our *worship,* of our prayers and hymns, not the neatly worked out formularies of theologians, actually determine what it is we say we believe. The old maxim is right: the way we pray does establish the way we believe. This is why changing the words of the prayer book raised the cry that the *theology* of our worship has been changed. There is a sense, of course, in which this is true. Since the worship expresses our theology any change in worship is bound to have some effect on it. But it is not true in the sense in which it is so often said: that the 1979 prayer book has radically altered the theology of the Episcopal Church. It would be more accurate to say that the way in which we *express* the theology of the Episcopal Church has been changing and developing throughout the years and centuries until many people came to feel uneasy with their worship precisely because it did *not* reflect the way they believed. Some prayers and hymns were an embarrassment to them, such as the petition in the Prayer for the Whole State of Christ's Church asking that "Christian rulers" would "administer justice, for the punishment of wickedness and vice, and the maintenance of [God's] true religion and virtue." At the very least, this sits badly with the Constitution of the United States! It is this that makes it continually necessary for us to find new images and figures in which to express our faith. The old words no longer say what we mean.

It is not that we proof text our theology from The Book of Common Prayer but rather that what we hear, say and do in our common worship have become the most natural way for us to express what we believe about God and about ourselves in relation to God. Whenever this stops happening we feel the tension and cry out for liturgical reform, or for a return to the religion expressed in the liturgy.

2
The Daily Offices

Morning and Evening Prayer as public services

Along with the weekly celebration of the eucharist on
Sunday the prayer book provides for the daily services of
Morning and Evening Prayer. These services trace their
origins through the early Church to the daily prayer services of the Jews.

It is uncertain exactly when the daily worship in the
synagogue, which is so prominent a feature of contemporary Judaism, began but daily prayer both in the home and
in the Temple were clearly a normal part of Jewish life in
the time of Christ. The devout Jew recited the *shema* three
times a day. (This is the credal confession beginning, "Hear,
O Israel: the Lord our God is the only Lord. Love the Lord
your God with all your heart, with all your soul, with all
your mind, and with all your strength." To this were added
various prayers and benedictions.) The earliest Christians
appear to have continued this pattern and, following the
command of Christ, made the Lord's Prayer the central
prayer of their devotions, reciting it thrice daily.

Wherever it was possible Christians gathered in groups
to pray in the morning and in the evening as did the Jews.
When Christianity became a legal religion in the fourth

century formal services of morning and evening prayer formed part of the worship of major churches. These services were characterized by the singing of psalms and other hymns in praise to God and by the offering of a common prayer by the assembly. The distinctive feature of evening prayer was the bringing in of a lighted lamp and the singing of a hymn to Christ as the light of the world. The hymn *Phos hilaron* in Evening Prayer in The Book of Common Prayer was already considered the traditional hymn for this purpose in the fourth century.

The services of Morning and Evening Prayer in the prayer book are the current forms of these ancient services of prayer. Their form is the result of the thorough revision by Archbishop Thomas Cranmer in the sixteenth century of the daily offices used in medieval monasteries. Subsequent revision has restored some ancient elements, such as the evening hymn *Phos hilaron* (which the monks left out) and shows the continuing attempts to demonasticize and return the offices to their original purpose as common prayers for the whole congregation.

While the prayer book provides psalms and lessons for the celebration of both Morning and Evening Prayer every day of the year, there are not many places where such a regimen is practical. We do not live in small villages clustered around their parish churches. Even if we wanted to, most of us could not gather for daily worship. Only seminaries, monasteries, convents and parishes large enough to have sufficient worshipers to find two or three to gather daily can even attempt the daily celebration of Morning and Evening Prayer. In most places the daily offices are not daily but occasional services. Sunday

Evensong, Morning Prayer before a mid-week meeting or Evening Prayer and sermon during Lent are more typical uses of the offices. In many parishes Morning Prayer is used on Sundays as the Liturgy of the Word, either as a part of the celebration of the Holy Eucharist or as a separate service, but it is used only one day.

The prayer book structure of both offices is the same. After an optional introduction, consisting of an opening sentence of scripture and a general confession and absolution, the congregation is called to worship with a versicle and response. In the morning this is, "Lord, open our lips," asking God to break the silence of the night by permitting us to sing his praise. In the evening, "O God, make speed to save us" invokes divine assistance as we begin our prayer.

The invitatory, a hymn of praise which is the opening act of worship of the office, is one of the traditional psalms: *Venite* (Psalm 95) or *Jubilate* (Psalm 100) in the morning, and the hymn *Phos hilaron* ("O Gracious Light") in the evening. At Evensong the invitatory may be accompanied by the ancient tradition of lighting the vesper light (which is a part of the Order from Evening). The reading, or more properly the singing, of the psalms follows. The psalms are, of course, hymns and singing is the most natural way in which to render them. They are also superb poetry which can stand without music.

From the monastic tradition came the custom of reading the scriptures at the offices and lessons from both the Old and New Testament are assigned by the prayer book lectionary. Provision is made for the use of three such lessons daily. The recommended structure is the use of an Old Testament lesson and one from the New Testament at

Morning Prayer and the other New Testament lesson at Evening Prayer, if both offices are celebrated daily. When a single office is used, three lessons may be read. This is customary when Morning Prayer is used for the Ministry of the Word on Sundays or holy days.

Each lesson is followed by the singing of a canticle, a scriptural hymn. (When three lessons are read, the gospel reading follows the second canticle and precedes the sermon and creed.) A table recommending different canticles for each day of the week is in The Book of Common Prayer (144-5). This table is, however, only useful when the office is said daily. When it is celebrated only occasionally appropriate sung canticles should be chosen.

Following the last lesson a sermon may be preached. A sermon is not an integral part of the office, and no previous prayer book has provided for one, but if a sermon is desired it follows the final reading and precedes the canticle (or the creed if it replaces the third lesson). Alternatively, a sermon may be preached after the office or at the time of the hymn or anthem after the collects. (BCP 142) When the office is used as the Liturgy of the Word on Sunday, a sermon will normally be included at one of these places.

The Apostles' Creed, the Lord's Prayer, responsive prayers called suffrages and appropriate collects conclude the office. The prayer book provides alternative sets of suffrages. One (A) is common to both Morning and Evening Prayer. The other (B) is proper to the time of day. The Lord's Prayer is the original final prayer of the office but the suffrages and proper collects were added in the middle ages as a fixed form of common prayer. More general prayers chosen by the officiant may follow. (These common prayers of the people are an original part of the office, but were detached from it in monastic use.)

The offices conclude with a traditional dismissal, "Let us bless the Lord," and a final scriptural sentence.

The offices are flexible in both structure and content and are an important part of Anglican liturgical practice and piety. In some places Morning Prayer has been used as the Ministry of the Word for the Sunday congregation. The Prayer Book clearly permits this, but expects that it will form a single service with the Holy Communion.

Noonday Prayer and Compline

Both of these offices have a long history in Christian practice but are new to The Book of Common Prayer. Noon was a traditional hour for Jewish and early Christian corporate prayer and Christians often prayed privately at that hour. (Acts 10 speaks of Peter praying on the roof at noon, for example.) There does not appear to have been any tradition of public Noonday Prayer until the rise of monasteries at which group prayer at noon usually preceded the common meal. Compline also finds its origin in monasteries as the dormitory prayers said before sleeping.

In providing these offices, The Book of Common Prayer was not attempting to add two new daily services but to provide forms for those occasions when it was desirable to have a service at those particular hours. In the monastic tradition not only noon but midmorning and midafternoon (the traditional breaks in the working day) were marked as hours of prayer (*Terce, Sext, and None*). The form of Noonday Prayer provided in The Book of Common Prayer has sufficient flexibility to permit its adaptation for all three hours of prayer. It can also be used for a simple and informal service at the lunch break of a meeting or during a quiet day. In a similar way Compline may be used at the close of an evening meeting, during a conference or retreat or as an occasional service of night prayers.

Either service may include hymns and sung psalms, and at Compline the *Nunc Dimittis* may be sung. Since both are essentially family prayers neither service requires an ordained officiant and both are often celebrated quite informally in ordinary rooms without the use of vestments.

The office as a model for private prayer

In addition to their use as public services the offices of The Book of Common Prayer are frequently recited by both clergy and laity as acts of private prayer. The prayer book provides a shortened form for this purpose which it calls "Daily Devotions for Individuals and Families." Both this and the fuller form provided for public celebration are widely used. Since the daily prayer of the church is the daily offices, it is not only reasonable but traditional that those who do not gather for daily celebrations make the offices models for their own prayers. In this way they are able to pray with the Church, making her prayer their own. Those who pray the office alone may describe themselves as participants in a great choir of all those throughout the Church who are praying the same prayers and reading the same lessons at the same hour. They may see their worship as part of the unceasing worship of the heavenly host. The use of the daily office makes private prayer more than personal. It is clearly not the same as the common celebration of Morning and Evening Prayer, but it has an aspect of common prayer about it, which is important to all Christians, since we pray not as individuals, but as members of the common body of the Church.

Those who use the daily offices as models for private prayer ought to remember that the services in the prayer book are public and their rubrics are intended for common celebration. They should feel free to alter and adapt these services to meet their own devotional needs, reading more or fewer psalms or lessons, omitting responsive sections, pausing to meditate on texts that strike them as significant.

3
The Sacrament of Christian Initiation

The central place of baptism in Christian Life

At the introduction to the renewal of baptismal vows in the Great Vigil of Easter, the celebrant says:

"Through the Paschal mystery, dear friends, we are buried with Christ by Baptism into his death, and raised with him to newness of life." (BCP 292)

This participation in the dying and rising again of Jesus is at the heart of Christian life and faith. It was this resurrection which the apostles proclaimed to the world and it is our sharing in it which makes us one with Christ. Baptism is the sacrament of our entrance into the paschal mystery. As St. Paul reminds us in *Romans* 6,

"Do you not know that all of us who have been baptized into Jesus Christ were baptized into his death? We were buried therefore with him by baptism into death, so that as Christ was raised from the dead by the glory of the Father, we too might walk in newness of life."

The prayer book expects that baptism will be administered in the context of "the Eucharist as the chief service on a Sunday or other feast" (BCP 298) and recommends that its celebration be confined to certain liturgically significant days during the year: the Great Vigil of Easter, Pentecost, All Saints, and the Baptism of our Lord. (BCP 312) In addition, baptism is a central theme in the liturgies for the seasons of Lent and Easter. Baptism is obviously intended to be a major event in the parish program and a significant occasion in the life of the congregation.

At the very least the Christian church has the same interest in the initiation of new members as any other society. Initiations are normally well-planned and well-attended events which are climaxes to the year's activities. This is what the prayer book expects Christian initiation to be. The incorporation of new members into the Body of Christ is a primary concern of the other members. It is central to the body's life and growth.

If participation in the resurrection is the central meaning of life in Christ, baptism shares in the centrality of the resurrection. It is our baptism which makes us members of that new people of God over whom the risen Christ is the Lord. And it is the regular participation of Christians in the celebration of that sacrament which is the means and occasions for the renewal of our common life in Christ and in the Church.

Baptism is, of course, also of crucial importance in the life of the individual Christian. But it is its communal and corporate meaning which is so often overlooked today. Our tendency is to make baptism a private sacrament, to treat it as solely the personal concern of the candidate's family.

For the individual Christian baptism means the appropriation of the redemption won by Christ for the entire human race. As the Catechism says,

"The inward and spiritual grace of Baptism is

union with Christ in his death and resurrection, birth into God's family the Church, forgiveness of sins, and new life in the Holy Spirit." (BCP 858)

At various times throughout its history the church has emphasized different aspects of baptismal grace: participation in the resurrection, membership in the church, forgiveness of sins, or new life in the Spirit. (When the majority of candidates were adults the forgiveness of sins and the beginning of a new life in the Spirit took on an importance they do not have in the baptism of infants. Today we are apt to be more concerned about union with Christ and membership in the church. In fact the exclusive emphasis on certain aspects of baptismal grace to the exclusion of others has often led to the rise of sects, either within the church or separate from it, sects who emphasized those things the rest of the church was neglecting.)

We who have been baptized live in the hope of the resurrection. The promise of our burial with Christ is in the water of our baptism. Christian initiation is not really an act, it is a process — the process of conversion by which we are brought out of error, darkness and death into light and life in Christ, passing over with him from the kingdom of Satan to the kingdom of God.

The theology of the baptismal liturgy

The principal place to find the teaching of the Episcopal Church concerning Christian initiation is in the baptismal liturgy. It is to baptism itself that we now turn our attention.

The first rubric under the heading "Concerning the Service" identifies baptism as the complete rite of Christian initiation and asserts that its effect is permanent:

"Holy Baptism is full initiation by water and the Holy Spirit into Christ's Body the Church. The bond which God establishes in baptism is indissoluble." (BCP 298)

It then sets the celebration within its proper context, at the Sunday eucharist, with the bishop or priest as the chief celebrant. This expresses the centrality of baptism in the life of the congregation and marks it as an act of the whole Church and not simply of the minister. It is the local church, assembled to make eucharist with its bishop or clergy, which celebrates the sacrament.

The structure of the celebration within the Sunday eucharist also tells us a good deal. The candidates are presented following the reading of the word of God and the sermon. Our action is in response to the divine initiative. Adult candidates are asked if they desire to be baptized. The godparents of children are asked to raise the child in "the Christian faith and life." (BCP 302) Baptism does not stand alone. It is a part, a central part, of the ongoing process of conversion and nurture.

The actions which follow are traditional and make manifest the meaning of what is being done. The candidates renounce evil and turn to Christ. (BCP 302f) They join with those already baptized in saying the Apostles' Creed, the ancient baptismal creed of the Western Church. The congregation offers prayer for them. By these actions the candidates are prepared to pass over with Christ from death to life. So to speak, they choose the side of Christ in the cosmic struggle, affirm the traditional faith of the church, and are surrounded and supported by the prayers of the people.

The Thanksgiving over the Water, which follows in the service, is the central prayer of the baptismal rite. It makes the most complete theological statement of what we are doing:

"In [the water of Baptism] we are buried with Christ in his death. By it we share in his resurrection. Through it we are reborn by the Holy Spirit. Therefore in joyful obedience to your Son, we bring into his fellowship those who come to him in faith, baptizing them in the Name of the Father, and of the Son, and of the Holy Spirit.

". . . we pray you, by the power of your Holy Spirit, that those who are here cleansed from sin and born again may continue for ever in the risen life of Jesus Christ our Savior." (BCP 306f)

Participation in the dying and rising of Jesus, new birth by the Holy Spirit and forgiveness of sins are, as we have already seen, the chief effects of baptism. They are clearly proclaimed in this central prayer of the baptismal liturgy.

The prayer for the Consecration of Chrism, said by the bishop after the Thanksgiving over the Water, in a similar way explains the meaning of anointing with oil:

". . . that those who are sealed with (this consecrated oil) may share in the royal priesthood of Jesus Christ . . ." (BCP 307)

At his baptism Christ was anointed by the Holy Spirit as the messiah. At ours we are anointed with oil that we may share in that royal priesthood. (The early Christians said that it is by virtue of this anointing that we are called Christians.)

The theologically weighty prayers are followed by the

appropriate sacramental actions: washing with water, signing with the cross, anointing with oil and laying on of hands. The last are accomplished in a single act in which a hand is placed on the newly baptized person's head and a cross is traced with oil on the forehead with the proclamation that he or she is "sealed by the Holy Spirit in Baptism and marked as Christ's own for ever." (BCP 308) These two actions are separated by a prayer which expounds their meaning:

"Heavenly Father, we thank you that by water and the Holy Spirit you have bestowed upon *these* your *servants* the forgiveness of sin, and raised *them* to the new life of grace. Sustain *them,* O Lord in your Holy Spirit. Give *them* an inquiring and discerning heart, the courage to will and to persevere, a spirit to know and to love you, and the gift of joy and wonder in all your works." (BCP 308)

In this prayer reference is make to the sevenfold gifts of the Holy Spirit which are bestowed on the initiates in the baptismal rite. The *seal of the Holy Spirit*, which is mentioned both at the signing with the cross and in the Consecration of Chrism, is an ancient expression which denoted the placing of God's seal or mark upon those who are his. It is the "brand" of the Good Shepherd of his own sheep, the seal of the heavenly king on the foreheads of his servants. The sign is, of course, the cross.

The service continues with the welcome of the newly baptized by the congregation as fellow members of the household of God and sharers in Christ's eternal priesthood. The new Christians are greeted with the kiss of peace and participate in the celebration of the Holy Eucharist, thereby exercising their new membership in the priestly people. (1 Peter 2)

We see in this rite a clear meaning and structure. The candidates renounce Satan and accept Christ. They are washed and signed with the cross. They are received by the congregation as fellow members of Christ's body, the church.

The place of confirmation in the process

The most obvious question raised by the prayer book's description of baptism as *full initiation* (BCP 298) is, "What then is the place of confirmation in the process of Christian initiation?" This question is best answered by a look at the confirmation service itself.

In this rite candidates reaffirm their renunciation of evil and renew their commitment to Jesus Christ. They renew their baptismal covenant, reciting again the Apostles' Creed. The bishop then prays:

"Almighty God, we thank you that by the death and resurrection of your Son Jesus Christ you have overcome sin and brought us to yourself, and that by the sealing of your Holy Spirit you have bound us to your service."

This is a summary of what happens in baptism. It gives thanks for what God has done for us in that sacrament. The prayer then continues:

"Renew in *these* your *servants* the covenant you made with *them* at *their* Baptism. Send *them* forth in the power of that Spirit to perform the service you set before *them* . . ." (BCP 418)

The bishop prays that God will renew the baptismal

30

covenant and send the candidates forth in the power of the Holy Spirit. This is the key to the understanding of confirmation. It is not a second stage in Christian initiation. It is a renewal and reaffirmation of what was done in baptism. This is reflected in the opening rubric of the service:

"In the course of their Christian development, those baptized at an early age are expected, when they are ready and have been duly prepared, to make a mature public affirmation of their faith and commitment to the responsibilities of their Baptism and to receive the laying on of hands by the bishop." (BCP 412)

Children have, of course, not been able to make the baptismal promises themselves. They have entered into the baptismal covenant through the actions of their parents and godparents. When these children are ready and able to make these promises themselves they are presented for confirmation. At this time they make their "mature public affirmation of faith and commitment" and receive the laying on of the bishop's hands. The clear implication of the prayer book's language is that they are no longer children but young adults capable of mature commitment. (Whether adolescents are sufficiently mature to be able to do this is a question which needs to be more fully discussed than it has generally been in the past.)

The place of confirmation in the initiation process for those who have been baptized as children is clear. It is a mature, adult act on their part, owning the faith into which they have been baptized and renewing their commitment to Christian life and service. God's part in the action is the renewal of the grace of the Holy Spirit. Following the bishop's prayer he lays hands on each candidate saying either the traditional formula:

"Defend, O Lord, your servant N., with your heavenly grace, that *he* may continue yours for ever, and daily increase in your Holy Spirit more and more, until *he* comes to your everlasting kingdom."

or this newly-composed one:

"Strengthen, O Lord, your servant N. with your Holy Spirit; empower *him* for your service; and sustain *him* all the days of *his* life." (BCP 418)

The traditional form speaks of the ongoing, strengthening power of the Holy Spirit which the candidate will receive throughout life. The newer form also speaks of empowerment for service. These are traditional Anglican confirmation themes. Neither imply that there is some fresh gift here bestowed which has not been given in baptism.

There is some confusion about the purpose of confirmation owing to the fact that the Episcopal Church formerly had a regulation forbidding the unconfirmed to receive Holy Communion. This practice in the Church of England goes back to a reform-minded, thirteenth century archbishop who wished to encourage his bishops to do more confirming. By requiring confirmation before communion he hoped that parents would bring pressure on the bishops to be more diligent and would themselves be encouraged to present their children. The purpose of the rubric was neither to exclude Protestants (of whom there were none in the thirteenth century) nor children (since confirmation was then normally administered to infants). This regulation was dropped by the Episcopal Church in 1970 and does not appear in the new prayer book.

Theologians objected to it because it seemed to make reception of Holy Communion a reward for faithful attendance at confirmation class or for learning the catechism. The expectation of the present prayer book is that all baptized Christians may receive Holy Communion.

The opening rubrics of the confirmation service refer also to the case of those baptized as adults. Adults who are baptized by the bishop receive no further rite on confirmation. Those who are baptized by the parish priest, however, should expect to be presented to the bishop for the laying on of hands. This is also true for those who have been baptized in other Christian churches and wish to become Episcopalians. Every member of the Episcopal Church is at some time personally presented to the bishop for the imposition of episcopal hands. (An alternative formula is provided for those being received from other churches. It recognizes that baptism has already made them members of the one holy catholic and apostolic church and that it is this communion into which they are being received by the bishop.)

Provision is made in the confirmation rite for another group as well: those who have already been baptized and confirmed but wish to make a public reaffirmation of their baptismal vows. These might be people who had been separated from the Church for many years or those who have had an experience which gives new meaning, depth and direction to their baptismal commitment. An alternative form to accompany the laying on of hands is provided.

Confirmation, as it is set forth in The Book of Common Prayer, has a number of important functions in the life of the congregation and its individual members. First, for those baptized as children it is the occasion for their owning their inherited faith. Second, for those coming into the Episcopal Church as adults it is the formal reception in this communion by the bishop. Finally, for those for whom church membership has acquired a new dimension it is an occasion of public renewal and reaffirmation. For all it is the renewal of the promise of the sacrament of Holy Baptism so that they may be strengthened by the Holy Spirit for God's service.

The Catechumenate

The catechumenate is described in *The Book of Occasional Services* as, "a period of training and instruction in Christian understandings about God, human relationships, and the meaning of life, which culminates in the reception of the Sacraments of Christian Initiation." (*BOS* 114) Its purpose is to be a rite of passage to bring one who is outside into the Christian fellowship. In an age in which an increasing number of candidates for baptism are adults who have been brought up without much knowledge of Christianity, this ancient structure for the Christian initiation of adults may more and more find a place in our practice. The process falls naturally into four stages which are outlined in *The Book of Occasional Services* with appropriate liturgical rites.

The first stage is *evangelization*. This is where the Christian gospel makes its first impact on the life of the non-Christian. He or she really hears the good news of Jesus Christ for the first time and is converted; that is, turned toward Jesus and an acceptance of new life in him. It is as a result of this process of evangelization that new people approach the church and inquire about the faith. When they come to the point of deciding to move ahead they are admitted as catechumens.

Admission to the Catechumenate marks the beginning of the second stage. It is a serious step but it is more like dating than marriage. It is an activity which involves the entire congregation. The inquirers stand before the congregation at a Sunday service and are asked to accept the Summary of the Law as a standard of life and to open their hearts and minds to receive the Lord Jesus. (*BOS* 117f) They also promise to be regular in attending worship and instruction. The congregation is asked to help them by prayer and example and a cross is marked on their foreheads.

The catechumenate might be described as a period of aculturation. It provides not only instruction but support for the convert. The catechumens are now formally associated with the Church and have an opportunity to participate regularly in worship and try to live a Christian life. Their formal instruction includes prayer, scripture and Christian living. They are members of the Christian community and are regularly prayed for by the congregation.

The catechumenate is fairly low key. The pivotal point comes when the catechumen is enrolled as a candidate for baptism. Traditionally this is done on the first Sunday in Lent or the first Sunday of Advent, with baptism at the Easter Vigil or Feast of the Baptism of our Lord as the goal.

Candidacy for baptism is the third stage. It is a period of intense preparation for baptism. It involves the whole congregation in public acts at the Sunday eucharist, and the individual candidates in fasting, examination of conscience and prayer, so that each may be spiritually ready for baptism.

The enrollment of candidates takes place at a public service. They write their names in the parish register and are supported by the prayers of the assembled congregation. (*BOS* 122ff) On the three Sundays before their baptism the candidates are called forward to kneel for the prayers and blessings of the Church. (*BOS* 124f) This is also a period of systematic instruction and spiritual preparation of the candidates. The traditional topics are Bible, creed and Lord's Prayer. The candidates learn and feel what it means to be a Christian.

The climax of this third stage is the celebration of Holy Baptism, at which the candidates receive Holy Communion and are welcomed as members of the Church of Jesus Christ and the local congregation. *Full membership in the Church* marks the transition to the fourth stage in which the Church assists the new Christians, ". . . to experience the fulness of the corporate life of the Church and to gain a deeper understanding of the meaning of the Sacraments" (*BOS* 116) which they have received.

Inevitably today some, perhaps even most, of those we reach with our programs of evangelism and outreach are already baptized. Many are already communicants. But their needs are the same as the unbaptized. They may possess some information but they need to be incorporated into the life of Christ and his church. This has been done for them in the sacrament of Holy Baptism but awareness has not been allowed to grow and ripen. It needs to be restored and renewed.

4
The Eucharist

Historical survey

We have already seen in the first chapter that the eucharist has been the center of Christian worship from the earliest times. Gregory Dix, in one of the truly memorable passages in his great book *The Shape of the Liturgy*, wrote:

"At the heart of it all is the eucharistic action, a thing of absolute simplicity — the taking, blessing, breaking, and giving of bread and the taking, blessing, and giving of a cup of wine, as these were first done by a young Jew before and after supper with His friends on the night before He died . . . He had told His friends to do this henceforward with the new meaning 'for the *anamnesis*' of Him, and they have done it always since." [743f]

This is almost literally what has happened. One of our earliest non-biblical accounts of Christian worship dates from the middle of the second century and describes what Christians do on Sundays in this way:

"On the day called Sunday there is a meeting in one place of those who live in cities or in the country, and the memoirs of the apostles (which are called

gospels) or the writings of the prophets are read as long as time permits. When the reader has finished, the president in a discourse urges and invites us to the imitation of these noble things. Then we also stand up together and offer prayers. And . . . when we have finished the prayer, bread is brought and wine and water, and the president likewise sends up prayers and thanksgivings to the best of his ability, and the congregation assents, saying the Amen; the distribution of the consecrated [elements] takes place and they are sent to the absent by the deacons."
(Justin Martyr, *1 Apology 67*)

Already by the second century the form of the Sunday service is that with which we are familiar: scripture readings, sermon, prayers, preparation of the gifts, Great Thanksgiving, Communion. The actions of Jesus at the last supper before and after the meal have been separated from the meal itself and combined into 1) taking the bread and wine, 2) giving thanks over them, 3) breaking the bread and 4) giving the bread and wine to the people: the familiar actions of 1) offertory, 2) consecration, 3) fraction and 4) communion which are found in all liturgies.

We do not know how these ritual actions came to be separated from the actual meal of which they were originally a part, but we do know that it happened everywhere in approximately the same way. The eucharistic actions were not, however, allowed to stand alone but were joined to a service of prayer and Bible reading derived ultimately from the worship of the synagogue. This produced the pattern with which we are familiar today.

When worship moved from the homes of individual

Christians into church buildings it became necessary to add entrance and exit ceremonies to the earlier structure in order to move the officiants in and out of the assembly rooms. This structure emerged:

entrance song (introit)
opening prayer (collect)
Old Testament reading (prophet)
Psalm (gradual)
New Testament reading (epistle)
gospel
sermon
prayers of the people
preparation of bread and wine (offertory)
great thanksgiving (eucharistic prayer)
breaking of bread (fraction)
communion
final prayer
dismissal

This outline, with the addition of singing during the gospel procession, the offertory, and communion (the times when there was action but no speaking), is the traditional structure of the Sunday eucharist.

One may say that the history of the eucharist after the development of this structure has been simply one of distortion and renewal. People lost their ability to participate because the language became foreign and then worship was restored to the vernacular; when liturgical roles were usurped by clergy and choirs, lay ministry and congregational singing were revived; the proclamation of the word was buried under a sacramentalism which verged on magic and then preaching was exalted to the virtual exclusion of sacramental worship before the balance was restored.

If this account seems to suggest that the contemporary liturgy is the crown and climax of all that went before, this too is an error. We can at least claim that we are once more following the main line in which the Sunday celebration is one of word and sacrament, with the full, informed, active participation of the whole people of God. The liturgy continues to grow and change with us as we grow into the fulness of Christ. Perhaps our concern today should be that so many of the people of God neither participate nor wish to participate in worship, while the rest of us gather exclusively in our own churches to celebrate similar services. Because we call ourselves by different denominational names we do not join to celebrate a common eucharist. The sacrament of unity in Christ divides us.

The liturgy of the Word of God

The first of the two interconnected parts of the eucharist, which the prayer book calls "The Word of God," is not simply a devotional preparation for Holy Communion but the Church's principal proclamation of the word. It is one of two coordinate elements in a normative act of worship. Its core is the reading and proclamation of the gospel of Jesus Christ.

The liturgy actually begins with an entrance song, either a hymn, psalm or anthem. This is more than incidental music during the entrance of the ministers: it serves to involve and unify the congregation by singing together. This leads the congregation to an opening acclamation and response, identifying the presiding minister or celebrant and putting the congregation in dialogue with him or her. (Obviously these goals are not met if the entrance song is sung only by a choir or the opening dialogue is with an assisting minister.)

At this point in the entrance rite we move either to a hymn of praise such as *Gloria in Excelsis* or to a penitential act with a general confession. Whichever choice is made, a tone, either festal or penitential, will be set for the service that follows. A third option for ordinary occasions includes an opening prayer, the Collect for Purity, followed by either the *Kyrie* ("Lord, have mercy") or the *Trisagion* ("Holy God, Holy and Mighty"). These are both ancient chants of praise but less obviously festive than the *Gloria*. The singing of one of these hymns concludes the entrance rite, whichever option is chosen.

The Liturgy of the Word begins with the ancient greeting, "The Lord be with you," again bringing the congregation into dialogue with the presiding minister, and the Collect of the Day. This short prayer sets a theme for the scripture readings which follow. On Sundays and major holy days three readings are provided. On weekdays there are usually only two. The number of readings, or lessons, has varied throughout Christian history but the gospel has always held the place of honor as the final reading.

The readings before this gospel are normally read by lay persons designated by the celebrant. (BCP 354) Reading the lessons is a lay ministry which was usurped by the clergy at a time when few lay people were able to read.

The first lesson is usually from the Old Testament and the second from the New. A psalm is sung or read between them. The psalm was once known as the gradual because it was lead by a cantor from the steps (or *grades*) of the lectern. It is a part of the readings for the day and should not be omitted. The hymn or anthem sung between the second lesson and the gospel is intended to accompany the moving of the gospel book to the lectern, pulpit, or the midst of the congregation where it is to be read.

The gospel is the chief reading. It is traditionally read by the deacon, but if there is no deacon it may be read by an assisting priest or by the celebrant. The people stand for the reading of the gospel as a mark of honor to the presence of Christ, revealed to his people in the words of the gospel. In the early church, lights and incense were carried before the gospel book, held aloft by the deacon to mark the real presence of Christ in the gospel.

The reading of the gospel is followed by a sermon, the discourse of the presiding minister, ". . . urging and inviting us to the imitation of these noble things," which has formed a part of both Jewish and Christian worship from ancient times. Jesus himself preached on the reading from Isaiah in the synagogue at Nazareth. St. Paul frequently was invited to preach in synagogues. The sermon follows the gospel reading since its purpose is to help the congregation to apply the gospel to their own lives.

On Sundays and holy days the Nicene Creed, the ecumenical symbol of the faith originally adopted by the Councils of Nicea and Constantinople in the fourth century, is recited as a response to the proclamation of the gospel. It is a witness to our continuity with the catholic church of the ages, to our unity of faith with those who have gone before us, a corporate affirmation of the faith of the church not an individual statement of belief. That is why it, like the prayers of the liturgy, is in the plural rather than the singular.

Corporate prayer is the liturgical response to the proclamation and hearing of the word. Like the second-century Christians, "We stand up together and offer prayers." The gathered church makes its common prayers for its many corporate and personal concerns. Following the prayers we greet one another in peace. The peace is the bridge between the word of God and the Holy Communion. If the general confession was not used at the beginning of the service it may form the concluding act of our common prayers and precede the expression of peace. The confession of sin is an integral part of our common prayer. The sixteenth-century invitation to communion, still a part of Rite One in our Book of Common Prayer, says, "Ye who do truly and earnestly repent you of your sins, and are in love and charity with your neighbors . . ." (BCP 330) This is expressed in the liturgy by the saying together of the general confession and the exchange of the peace.

Placing the peace between the prayers of the people and the preparation of the bread and wine was common in the early church. In this position it forms a bridge between the two parts of the service. It also corresponds to the teaching of Matthew 5:23-4:

"If you are offering your gift at the altar, and there remember that your brother has something against you, leave your gift before the altar and go; first be reconciled to your brother and then come and offer your gift."

The inclusion of this passage among the offertory sentences in the prayer book (BCP 376) leaves little doubt

43

that this connection was seen by those who compiled our present service. The greeting of one another in peace symbolizes our being "in love and charity" so that we may presume to offer our gifts at the altar as neighbors.

The liturgy of the Holy Communion

The Holy Communion, the second part of the eucharist, begins with the preparation of the gifts of bread and wine and placing of them on the altar. This is traditionally called the offertory. It is an action, not a set of words. Frequently a hymn or an anthem, also called the offertory, is sung during this time.

The bread and wine are brought forward by representatives of the congregation along with money and other gifts. They are presented to the deacon or the celebrant who "sets the table" for the sacred meal placing the bread on an appropriate plate and the wine mixed with water in a cup.

The Great Thanksgiving is the central prayer of the service. It is offered by the presiding minister, in our tradition always a priest or bishop. Its origin is in the prayer of thanksgiving said by our Lord over the cup at the conclusion of the last supper. The name eucharist, as a title for the service, is derived from the Great Thanksgiving: Eucharist is the Greek word for *thanksgiving*.

A variety of eucharistic prayers are used in the Episcopal Church but all express the same themes. Most follow the same outline, filling it out with different words. The traditional outline was adopted by the first American Book of Common Prayer from the Scottish Episcopalians who adapted it from the eucharistic prayers of the ancient church. It begins, like the Liturgy of the Word, with a dialogue between the celebrant and the congregation. "The Lord be with you. Lift up your hearts. Let us give thanks." (BCP 361) These are the invitations which the priest extends, asking the whole people of God to join in the eucharistic action.

First the eucharistic prayer gives thanks to God. Often this takes the form of proper prefaces which vary from season to season. One appointed for ordinary Sundays prays,

> "It is right and a good and joyful thing, always and everywhere to give thanks to you, Father Almighty, Creator of heaven and earth.

> "Through Jesus Christ our Lord; who on the first day of the week overcame death and the grave, and by his glorious resurrection opened to us the way of everlasting life." (BCP 361, 377)

Other prefaces give thanks for specific things proper to the occasion being celebrated. In all cases they conclude by asking us to join with the heavenly choir in singing the angelic hymn of "Holy, holy, holy."

After the *Sanctus*, the thanksgiving continues, thanking God for our creation and redemption through Jesus Christ. The thanksgiving for redemption concludes with the narrative of the institution of the eucharist at the last supper, including the words of Christ over the bread and cup and the command, "Do this for the remembrance of me."

The repetition of Christ's command provides the transition from the recounting of the might acts of God to our present action. In the paragraph called the *anamnesis* or the *oblation* we offer to God the bread and cup, remembering (which is what *anamnesis* means) the saving acts of Jesus Christ. "Recalling his death, resurrection, and ascension, we offer you these gifts." (BCP 363)

The *epiclesis* or *invocation* then asks the Holy Spirit to descend upon us and upon the bread and wine, "that they may be the Sacrament of the Body of Christ and his Blood of the new Covenant" (BCP 369) and that we may be united with him. The prayer concludes with a *doxology*, to which we, like the early Christians, reply *Amen*.

The participation of the congregation (in the opening dialogue, in the *Sanctus*, in the *Amen* and in other places) signify that this is not the personal prayer of the celebrant but is offered by the priest as the one presiding over the assembly of the faithful. It is the prayer of the whole people of God. The eucharist is the offering not of the priest but of the body of Christ, the Church united with her divine head in his self-offering to the Father.

At the end of the eucharistic prayer all join in saying the Lord's Prayer. In Christ, "we are bold to say, Our Father." It is the natural climax of our participation in Christ's self-offering. Again it binds the congregation together at a focal point in the celebration, expressing our unity with one another in Christ, praying as he taught us. The petition, "Give us this day our daily bread," has been seen from early times as preparation for receiving communion and was apparently the original reason for the inclusion of the Lord's Prayer in the service between the thanksgiving and communion.

The breaking of bread is primarily a utilitarian action. A loaf of bread must be broken in order to be shared. In

Jewish tradition the bread over which thanks has been given is immediately broken and shared; it was this tradition which Jesus followed at the last supper. Christians have often seen in the breaking of the bread a symbol of the breaking of the Lord's body on the cross and of the necessity of our being broken in order to share our life in Christ. One of the earliest Christian eucharistic prayers, preserved in our hymnal, includes this petition:

"As grain, once scattered on the hillsides,
Was in this broken bread made one,
So from all lands thy Church be gathered
Into thy kingdom by thy Son."
(from the *Didache*, tr. F. Bland Tucker)

The breaking of the bread is followed by the reception of communion. The receiving of the bread and wine over which thanks have been given is the effective sign of our participation in Christ's sacrifice, eating his body and drinking his blood. The name *Holy Communion* indicates the entire service, for it is in receiving communion that we are most closely united with Christ in his saving acts of dying and rising again. Once in baptism, and week by week in the eucharist, we are united with the crucified and risen Lord.

A single post-communion prayer and the dismissal of the people conclude the service. For many centuries the presiding minister has given a concluding blessing. The bishop still does so and priests may do so. The blessing arose in a period when most lay people seldom received communion and there are those today who consider it redundant to follow Christ's great blessing with that of a minister. The dismissal sends the congregation forth into the world to be the church.

Its central place in theology and practice

The eucharist in Christian tradition and in The Book of Common Prayer is the chief act of worship on the Lord's day and the climax and conclusion of the sacrament of Christian initiation. Like baptism it is a participation in the death and resurrection of the Lord. Every Sunday is a celebration of the resurrection and it is the Sunday eucharist which gives to the Lord's day its paschal character, just as it is the resurrection which provides the context for the eucharist. This does not mean that the church can never do anything else but celebrate the eucharist. But it is when we celebrate the eucharist that the church most clearly acts as the Body of Christ. Non-eucharistic services, both the Daily Offices and occasional Pastoral Offices, provide the background and context for the great gospel sacrament.

If the eucharist is the most characteristic act of the church, the nature of that Church is most clearly manifested when the bishop presides. We are an Episcopal Church and bishops are not, in spite of appearances sometimes, bureaucrats and administrators but priests and pastors. As the prayer book says,

"It is the bishop's prerogative, when present, to be the principal celebrant at the Lord's Table, and to preach the Gospel." (BCP 354)

But the eucharist is not the action of one person, not even of the bishop. It is the action of the Body of Christ, head and members. That means that Christ is the principal actor and we all in our various ministries play our own parts:

lay persons, priests, deacons and bishops, offering "the Church's sacrifice of praise and thanksgiving [as] the way by which the sacrifice of Christ is made present and in which he unites us to his one offering of himself." (BCP 859)

5
The Liturgical Year

When we open the prayer book we find that the first section following the preface and general instructions is The Calendar of the Church Year (BCP 15ff) and a more extensive look informs us that a total of 157 pages out of 1001 are devoted to material related to the year. When we attend the Episcopal Church we are continually confronted with references to seasons, times, holy days and the like. The effect of all this should be to convince us of the importance of the liturgical year to the Episcopal Church!

Sunday and the Christian week

At the heart of the liturgical year is the Christian week and the celebration of the Lord's day, Sunday. Our ecclesiastical week is a contribution of Judaism to the world. The Jewish week is dominated by its seventh day, Saturday, the sabbath.

Christians continued to observe the Jewish week but gave it a new focus. The first day of the week was celebrated as the Lord's day. It was the day on which Jesus rose from the dead and appeared to his disciples. It was the day on which he was known to them in the breaking of bread at the supper at Emmaus. It was the day on which the Holy Spirit descended in tongues of fire upon the apostles. It was also the day, according to a second century writer (Justin Martyr, *1 Apology 67*), "on which God transforming darkness and matter made the universe." From apostolic times it has been the day on which the Lord's people gather to celebrate the Lord's supper, the holy eucharist.

The prayer book says, "All Sundays of the year are feasts of our Lord Jesus Christ" (BCP 16) and describes the day as "the weekly remembrance of the glorious resurrection of your Son our Lord." (BCP 98) It is the principal Christian festival, and only the major feasts of our Lord are allowed to take precedence over its celebration.

The prayer book mentions another weekly observance which is dependent on the weekly celebration of the Lord's day. Fridays, except those during festive seasons, are to be observed as days of special devotion "in commemoration of the Lord's crucifixion." (BCP 17) The observance is to be "by special acts of discipline and self-denial." The traditional way of observing Friday is by fasting or abstaining from eating meat, but the prayer book leaves the way open for almost any sort of special devotional observance. As Sunday is observed as the resurrection festival so Friday is commemorated as the day of the crucifixion. It is this alternation of feast and fast which is characteristic of the liturgical year.

Easter, the feast of feasts

As the resurrection is central to Christian faith the festival of the resurrection is central to the liturgical year. In its weekly form, the Lord's day, it is the great occasion of

Christian worship. In its annual form, Easter, it dominates the yearly cycle. Sunday is often described as a little easter, but it would be more accurate to call Easter a big Sunday for in the Easter festival the dying and rising of Jesus Christ and our death and resurrection in him is proclaimed and celebrated.

Easter is not the celebration of a single day. It is a season of seven weeks, the 'great fifty days.' It is preceded by the solemn commemoration of the passion of Christ in Holy Week. The Great Vigil is the chief Easter celebration. Baptism is the sacrament of our entrance into the paschal mystery and the eucharist is the sacrament of our participation in it. They are related to each other as birth is related to life. Their celebration at the Great Vigil is the fullest proclamation of this saving mystery. The celebrant says to the congregation at the renewal of baptism vows in the vigil,

"Through the Paschal mystery, dear friends, we are buried with Christ by Baptism into his death, and raised with him to newness of life." (BCP 292)

This is the essence of the Easter proclamation. We are united with Christ in his death and resurrection. The service itself expresses this with dramatic simplicity. A great light, the paschal candle, is kindled so that we may see to read and pray throughout the night. The Bible is read and prayer and praise is offered, culminating in the proclamation of the resurrection and its sacramental celebration in baptism and the eucharist.

The Great Vigil begins with the proclamation of the light of Christ and the lighting of a new fire. The large candle symbolizes the breaking in of the light of Christ to the world of sin and death. As the poetic *Exsultet*, the hymn of praise over the freshly lighted candle, expresses it,

"This is the night, when all who believe in Christ are delivered from the gloom of sin, and are restored to grace and holiness of light.

"This is the night, when Christ broke the bonds of death and hell, and rose victorious from the grave.

"How wonderful and beyond our knowing, O God, is your mercy and loving-kindness to us, that to redeem a slave you gave a Son.

"How holy is this night, when wickedness is put to flight, and sin is washed away. It restores innocence to the fallen, and joy to those who mourn. It casts out pride and hatred, and brings peace and concord.

"How blessed is this night, when earth and heaven are joined and man is reconciled to God." (BCP 287)

This great song of praise to Jesus Christ, the victorious king and true paschal lamb who has scattered darkness with his own conquering light, gathers images from scripture and Christian tradition and weaves them into a great paean of praise. It lifts the worshippers from the prosaic language of everyday life into the presence of the mystery of Jesus' dying and rising again of which we are made partakers.

The readings and collects tell afresh the story of salvation and our incorporation in it: creation, the flood, the binding of Isaac, the exodus, and finally the gospel of the resurrection. The epistle, the classic Pauline passage on baptism from Romans 6, ends, "You also must consider yourselves dead to sin and alive to God in Christ Jesus."

(Romans 6:11) The reading is followed by the Easter shout of *Alleluia!* putting the baptismal process into the context of our participation in the resurrection. The gospel (Matthew 28:1-10) provides the scriptural climax as the service moves to the celebration of the Easter sacraments.

The meaning of the Easter festival is well expressed in another of the Easter collects:

"Almighty God, who through your only-begotten Son Jesus Christ overcame death and opened to us the gate of everlasting life: Grant that we, who celebrate with joy the day of the Lord's resurrection, may be raised from the death of sin by your life-giving Spirit." (BCP 222)

Throughout the great fifty days of the Easter season, ending on the day of Pentecost, these themes are renewed and represented to us so that the saving acts of God in Christ are proclaimed and make accessible to us in both word and sacrament. This is the church's greatest celebration, the festival of the resurrection.

Times and seasons

"The Church Year consists of two cycles of feasts and holy days." (BCP 15) These two cycles are interrelated and interconnected and it is their interplay which creates the liturgical year. The first is the Easter cycle. It consists of Lent, Holy Week, Easter, the fifty days of Eastertide and Pentecost. The second cycle is the Christmas cycle consisting of Advent, Christmas, Epiphany and the baptism of our Lord. The rest of the year, about half of it, often called Green Sundays, is made up of the seasons after the Epiphany and after Pentecost.

Both of the major cycles include a season of preparation, a major feast day and a festival season following it. Both are traditional times for the preparation of catechumens and the celebration of baptism. The baptism of our Lord, Easter and Pentecost are the oldest Christian baptismal days. Advent and Lent are the seasons of preparation, times of renewal for the entire congregation. Christmas and Easter are the great festivals and Epiphany and Pentecost are the feasts which bring the festival seasons to a close. (The baptism of Christ, the Sunday after Epiphany, moves the closing celebration of the Christmas season to a Sunday and provides a more suitable occasion than Christmas to celebrate baptisms.)

Another theologically significant way to look at the liturgical year is to think of it as two halves divided by the Day of Pentecost. The first half of the year celebrates the mighty acts of God from the first Advent to Pentecost through the events in the life of Christ. The second half of the year is the time of the Church extending from the Day of Pentecost to the following or second Advent, "until his coming again." It is this period in which we actually live and carry on the ministry and mission of Christ while in the celebration of the feasts and fasts of the liturgical year the mighty acts of God are made present in and for us. The prayer book says in the Christmas collect, "You have caused *this holy night* to shine with the brightness of the true Light" (BCP 212, italics are author's) and in the Pentecost collect, "*on this day* you opened the way of eternal life to every race and nation by the promised gift of your Holy Spirit." (BCP 227, italics are author's) The Great Vigil of Easter uses the phrase *this night* several times in describing what God has done. The liturgical year is not simply a teaching aid or lesson plan; in its specific temporality it is a celebration of the saving acts of God who comes to save us ". . . now in the time of this mortal life." (BCP 211)

Holy Days

In addition to the seasons of the Church year, the prayer book calendar includes the festivals of saints. The prayer book itself provides no explanation for the inclusion of these festivals but *Lesser Feasts and Fasts* contains this statement:

"Since the triumphs of the saints are a continuation and manifestation of the Paschal victory of Christ, the celebration of saints' days is particularly appropriate during this season" (i.e. Eastertide; *LFF* 56).

This theological statement is both traditional and significant for it places the celebration of the festivals of the saints in the context of the paschal mystery of Christ. The prayer book itself expresses this vision in the collect for St. Philip and St. James which contains the petition, "Grant that we, being mindful of their victory of faith, may glorify in life and death the Name of our Lord Jesus Christ." (BCP 240)

Another aspect of the celebration of the festivals of saints is expressed in the All Saints' Day collect which speaks of God as having, "knit together [his] elect in one communion and fellowship in the mystical body of [his] Son . . ." (BCP 245) We usually speak of this as the communion of saints. The implications of this belief are most fully drawn out in a collect from the burial service:

> "We pray that, encouraged by their examples, aided by their prayers, and strengthened by their fellowship, we also may be partakers of the inheritance of the saints in light . . ." (BCP 504)

The scriptural image behind the collect is that of Hebrews 12 which speaks of the saints as "a cloud of witnesses." We are one with them in the body of Christ in a fellowship of love and prayer.

The prayer book calendar contains two types of festivals of saints: major and lesser feasts. Traditionally the major feasts are called red letter days and the lesser feasts black letter days. This follows the customs of calendar makers who print holidays in red and other commemorations in black. The prayer book provides proper collects, psalms and lessons for the celebration of the eucharist and the Daily Offices for the red letter days. Collects, psalms and lessons for the celebration of the eucharist on black letter days are in the supplementary book, *Lesser Feasts and Fasts*. The collects, psalms and lessons proper to particular liturgical days are collectively known as *the propers*.

Unlike the red letter days which are celebrated throughout the Episcopal Church the celebration of the lesser feasts is optional and congregations may decide which, if any, of them they wish to observe. Not all will be relevant to every parish but as a group they remind us that sainthood did not cease with the New Testament era. Every age has produced its saints to join the "cloud of witnesses."

Significance of the calendar for Christian life

Probably the major significance of the calendar for Christian living is that it forces us to take time seriously. Unlike religions which seek to abolish time, Christianity seeks to redeem time. The mighty acts of God take place not in a fairy tale once-upon-a-time but within historical time. Those biblical events which underlie our faith, the Exodus, the incarnation and the resurrection were historical events which we believe have changed history. God brought Israel out of Egypt and established a special relationship with a particular people. God sent his son into the world where he lived and died and rose again. These events took place at a particular time and place yet their meaning for us transcends time. It is because God has done these things for us that we are Christians. We celebrate them not simply as historical events of a distant past but as the very events which make us who we are. It is these events in which the calendar immerses us. As Christians we find ourselves living in the present with our roots fixed in the past and our gaze turned to the future. As we say in the eucharistic liturgy:

"Christ has died.

Christ is risen.

Christ will come again." (BCP 363)

We celebrate in the present the mighty acts of God in Christ and look expectantly forward to their final fulfillment in what we call the second Advent.

The calendar also provides within our lives the alternating of feasts and fasts which is essential to balance. The weekly alternation of Friday and Sunday and the seasonal variation from Advent to Christmas, from Lent

58

to Easter, keep us from becoming one-sided in our religious life. It opens to us the events of the life of Christ and our participation in them in the church over the period of the year. It does this not by presenting us with a set of vignettes in the life of Jesus but by holding before us the mystery of salvation and turning it like a finely faceted jewel to reveal its ever-changing depths and colors so that we may live in its reflected and refracted light.

6
The Pastoral Offices

In addition to the gospel sacraments of baptism and eucharist and the Daily Offices, The Book of Common Prayer contains a number of rites for particular occasions in the lives of individual Christians. These too are common prayer for they are occasions in which the local congregation as the representatives of the whole church are involved in significant events in the lives of their individuals. They cover the span of an individual's life from "Thanksgiving for the Birth or Adoption of a Child" to "An Order for Burial." We have already discussed one of these rites, confirmation. We shall look at four others: marriage, reconciliation, ministry to the sick and funerals.

The Celebration and Blessing of a Marriage

"Christian marriage," according to the prayer book, "is a solemn and public covenant between a man and a woman in the presence of God." (BCP 422) It is not a ceremony which a minister performs but a unique relationship into which a man and woman enter. The role of the presiding priest or bishop is to witness their vows to each other as they enter this relationship, to pronounce the "nuptial blessing," and to celebrate the eucharist.

The celebration of the eucharist at a wedding is one of the oldest Christian traditions. At one time, and in many countries it is still the practice, Christians were married by the civil authorities and then came to the church to celebrate their marriage by participating together in the eucharist and receiving the church's blessing. At the eucharist the couple bring up the gifts to the altar and receive communion together, putting their new life into the context of the common life of the church as it lives that life in Christ.

The Episcopal Church does not require Episcopalians to celebrate their marriages in the church. A form for "The Blessing of a Civil Marriage" (BCP 433f) provides for the giving of the nuptial blessing and the celebration of the nuptial eucharist for couples who are already married.

The opening address of the prayer book service expresses well the Episcopal Church's teaching about marriage:

"The bond and covenant of marriage was established by God in creation . . . It signifies to us the union between Christ and his Church . . .

"The union of husband and wife in heart, body, and mind is intended by God for their mutual joy; for the help and comfort given one another in prosperity and adversity; and when it is God's will, for the procreation of children and their nurture in the knowledge and love of the Lord." (BCP 423)

These traditional statements have been revised from their form in the first English Book of Common Prayer which took them from even older English marriage rites.

The English *Alternative Service Book 1980* has treated them somewhat differently and a comparison of the two versions may deepen our understanding of the purposes of marriage:

"It is God's purpose that, as husband and wife give themselves to each other in love throughout their lives, they shall be united in that love as Christ is united with his Church. Marriage is given, that husband and wife may comfort and help each other, living faithfully together in need and in plenty, in sorrow and in joy. It is given, that with delight and tenderness they may know each other in love, and through the joy of their bodily union, may strengthen the union of their hearts and lives. It is given, that they may have children and be blessed in caring for them and bringing them up in accordance with God's will, to his praise and glory." (*ASB* 288)

After this introductory statement of what is involved the couple publicly declare their consent to the marriage, are prayed for in a collect, and listen to the scripture lessons. They then exchange their marriage vows and rings "as a symbol of my vow." (BCP 427) The prayers and blessing, the priest's contribution to the celebration, follow.

The exchange of the peace, from which the kiss between the bride and groom has remained traditional even though it has lost its meaning in the kiss of peace, either concludes the celebration or serves as a bridge to the eucharistic celebration as it does at other times. It recognizes within the Christian community the new status of the couple as husband and wife and celebrates it.

The rite in the prayer book accurately calls itself "The

Celebration and Blessing of a Marriage" and it is this involvement of the church in the marriage of Christians which has been a part of our heritage since the early centuries. It is a witness both to the couple and to the congregation of the meaning of Christian marriage and of what is important and enduring in its celebration.

The Reconciliation of Penitents

The Reconciliation of Penitents is new to the American Book of Common Prayer. The English prayer book has always contained a form of absolution to be used after private confession, but the form was omitted from the first American prayer book. The English form has nevertheless been widely used in the Episcopal Church.

The theology of this rite is most clearly expressed in its prayers and in the directions, "Concerning the Rite":

"The ministry of reconciliation, which has been committed by Christ to his Church, is exercised through the care each Christian has for others, through the common prayer of Christians assembled for public worship, and through the priesthood of the Church and its ministers declaring absolution." (BCP 446)

What follows in the prayer book, then, is one form of the exercise of this ministry. In other forms it is exercised by all Christians as in the general confession and other penitential rites of our public services. The individual use of this ministry of absolution is mentioned in the Exhortation (BCP 317) which has been a part of the Anglican eucharist since 1549. The form in the present prayer book reads,

"And if, in your preparation [for communion] you need help and counsel, then go and open your grief to a discreet and understanding priest and confess your sins, that you may receive the benefit of absolution, and spiritual counsel and advice; to the removal of scruple and doubt, the assurance of pardon, and the strengthening of your faith."

It is for this purpose that the rite, The Reconciliation of a Penitent, is provided. Two equivalent forms are given. The first is simple, direct and similar to the forms widely used by Episcopalians throughout the years. The second is based on Eastern Orthodox forms and sets sin and forgiveness in a larger framework, that of the baptismal life in Christ.

"Through the water of baptism you clothed me with the shining garment of [Christ's] righteousness, and established me among your children in your kingdom. But I have squandered the inheritance of your saints, and have wandered far in a land that is waste . . . I turn to you in sorrow and repentance. Receive me again into the arms of your mercy, and restore me to the blessed company of your faithful people; through him in whom you have redeemed the world." (BCP 450)

Reconciliation is a restoration of the relationship with Christ which has been established in baptism. The baptismal bond cannot be broken (BCP 298), but we can and do squander and waste our baptismal inheritance. Reconciliation celebrates our return to that relationship. Like the father in the parable of the prodigal son, God receives us into the arms of his mercy and restores us to the new life in Christ which we have rejected through sin. The image of the return of the prodigal is continued in the final dismissal:

"Now there is rejoicing in heaven; for you were lost, and are found; you were dead and are now alive in Christ Jesus our Lord." (BCP 451)

Reconciliation is a reestablishing of the Christian community with us returned as members. It involves a conversion, a turning again to Christ and a renewal of the baptismal covenant. Reconciliation is therefore closely related to the gospel sacraments of baptism and eucharist which are themselves means by which the saving death and resurrection of Jesus Christ reconcile us to God and to one another.

In the rite the penitent confesses to God in the presence of the priest, "all the serious sins troubling the conscience" and the confessor, "gives such counsel and encouragement as are needed and pronounces absolution." (BCP 446) Two alternative forms of absolution are provided. The first is that from the English prayer book:

"Our Lord Jesus Christ, who has left power to his Church to absolve all sinners who truly repent and believe in him, of his great mercy forgive you all your offenses; and by his authority committed to me, I absolve you from all your sins: In the Name of the Father, and of the Son, and of the Holy Spirit." (BCP 448)

This form has been widely used by Episcopalians for many years and makes it clear that the priest acts not on his own authority but in obedience to the command of Jesus Christ, who has given power "to his ministers to declare and pronounce to his people, being penitent, the absolution and remission of their sins." (BCP 269) The confession is made to God who alone can forgive sin; the priest acts only as the minister of Christ.

The second form is a translation by Massey Shepherd of a revised form developed by the Roman Concilium after Vatican Council II. It is not, unfortunately, the form which the Roman Catholics finally adopted. Its strength is that it makes clear that it is Jesus himself, and not the priest, who forgives sins.

"Our Lord Jesus Christ, who offered himself to be sacrificed for us to the Father, and who conferred power on his Church to forgive sins, absolve you through my ministry by the grace of the Holy Spirit, and restore you to the perfect peace of the Church." (BCP 451)

The prayer book also recognizes that another Christian who is not a priest may be asked to hear a confession. It requires that a confessor who is not a priest make it clear to the penitent that absolution will not be pronounced and provides a declaration of forgiveness which may be used. (BCP 446)

Christians do hear the confessions of other Christians. Parents hear the confessions of their children. Friends hear the confessions of friends. Holy men and women, whether ordained or lay, have always been sought out by those desiring spiritual guidance and counsel. The prayer book simply recognizes this and provides a prayer for lay confessors to use. It is one way in which the Church traditionally continues our Lord's ministry of reconciliation.

Finally, the prayer book teaches that whether the

confessor is a priest or lay person, "The secrecy of a confession is morally absolute for the confessor, and must under no circumstances be broken." (BCP 446) This rule, often called the seal of the confessional, protects the penitent. It prohibits the confessor from making any use of information gained as Christ's minister of reconciliation.

Ministration to the Sick

The ministry to the sick was central to the ministry of Jesus and is an integral part of the ministry the church exercises in his name. Too often the church has narrowed its ministry exclusively to the dying and has not taken seriously the possibility that those to whom it ministered might recover. The theological thrust of the Ministration to the Sick in the prayer book is healing. It is assumed that it is in this way that we continue the ministry of our Lord.

The prayer book provides a framework in which every sort of ministry to the sick person might be provided without expecting that all will be used at the same time. First it suggests scripture passages which may be read by or to the sick person by anyone with the time and ability to read. The passages speak of the love and healing power of God. If the sick person wishes to make a confession the form for The Reconciliation of a Penitent may follow the Bible readings or the general confession may be used. Human beings are complex creatures of body, mind and spirit and healing must encompass all aspects of the person. Forgiveness of sin is an integral part of the healing process and the sick person must be given an opportunity to deal with the sense of sin and separation.

Second the prayer book provides for laying on of hands

and anointing. This is the principal healing ministry of the Episcopal Church. Following the example of the apostolic church (James 5:14-16; Mark 6:7, 12-13) we lay healing hands upon the heads of the sick and anoint them with oil in the name of the Lord. The meaning of the laying on of hands is well expressed in one of the forms which accompanies the action:

". . .beseeching our Lord Jesus Christ to sustain you with his presence, to drive away all sickness of body and spirit, and to give you that victory of life and peace which will enable you to serve him both now and evermore." (BCP 456)

In a similar way the prayer for blessing the oil for the anointing of the sick sets it in a scriptural context:

". . . as your holy apostles anointed many that were sick and healed them, so may those who in faith and repentance receive this holy unction be made whole." (BCP 455)

An additional prayer following the anointing, based on the prayer in the 1549 English prayer book, speaks of the sacramental nature of the rite:

"As you are outwardly anointed with this holy oil, so may our heavenly Father grant you the inward anointing of the Holy Spirit. Of his great mercy, may he forgive you your sins, release you from suffering, and restore you to wholeness and strength. May he deliver you from all evil, preserve you in all goodness, and bring you to everlasting life." (BCP 456)

The inward anointing of the Holy Spirit is the spiritual grace of which the oil is outward and visible sign and we ask that release from suffering, forgiveness, and restoration to wholeness may be the effect. The oil is blessed by a priest. When necessary, deacons or lay persons may perform the anointing. (BCP 456)

Third, Holy Communion for the sick may take the form of a celebration at the bedside or the elements may be administered from the reserved sacrament. Communion of the sick from the elements consecrated at the Sunday eucharist is not only more convenient in many cases but it permits the sick person to share in the parish celebration from which he or she is unavoidably absent. It binds the sick person to the eucharistic life of the congregation.

These rites are intended for all who are sick. Separate provision is made for ministry to the dying: a beautiful Litany at the Time of Death (BCP 462ff) and commendatory prayers. (BCP 464f)

The Burial of the Dead

The baptized Christian is buried from the church, taking his or her place for the last time with the worshipping congregation. If the departed Christian is a communicant and a priest is available the eucharist is normally celebrated. If a deacon or lay reader must preside only the Liturgy of the Word is used. It is the Church's leave-taking of its departed member. The service itself is intended to be the Church's normal act of worship with prayers and lessons appropriate to the occasion. It expresses our joy that, "Because Jesus was raised from the dead, we too shall be raised," and our sorrow that we are parted from our loved one in death. (BCP 507) It is an Easter liturgy. Our mixed feelings of joy and sorrow are admirably expressed in the anthem in the commendation that concludes the service in the church. It includes the lines, "All of us go down to the dust, yet even at the grave we make our song: Alleluia, alleluia, alleluia." (BCP 499)

The prayer book recognizes that there are differing customs concerning the burial of the dead. It provides, for example, for the possibility that the burial may already have taken place (BCP 468) or that it may be pastorally desirable to provide a different type of funeral service. (BCP 506) Both traditional and contemporary forms of the service are included and there are many possible variations within the service.

When the body of the departed Christian is brought to the church a member of the congregation may lead the procession carrying the lighted paschal candle. (BCP 467) This symbol of the resurrection of Christ casts its light over the entire service which is literally conducted in the light of the resurrection. This procession may take place either at the beginning of the funeral or earlier. Prayers for a vigil or wake, are suggested (BCP 465) and these may be used either in the church or at a home where the body has been prepared.

Before the funeral service the coffin is closed and may be covered with a pall. A pall is a cloth, usually marked with a cross or other symbols of the resurrection, which conceals either the simplicity or the costliness of the casket. All of us are presented as equal before the Lord.

The traditional anthem sung at the beginning of the service is, "I am Resurrection and I am Life, says the Lord" (BCP 491) although other suitable hymns or anthems are frequently substituted. Like the paschal candle, the anthem sets the Easter tone of the liturgy.

The Church's resurrection faith is forcefully expressed in the prayers and scripture readings of the service, as, for example, in this collect:

"O God, who by the glorious resurrection of your Son Jesus Christ destroyed death, and brought life and immortality to light: Grant that your servant N., being raised with him, may know the strength of his presence, and rejoice in his eternal glory." (BCP 493)

After the scripture readings and the homily, which may be given by a friend or family member, the Apostles' Creed is recited "In the assurance of eternal life given at Baptism." (BCP 496)

The Prayers of the People mingle the themes of resurrection joy and mourning for the loss of a loved one.

"You wept at the grave of Lazarus, your friend; comfort us in our sorrow.

"You raised the dead to life; give to our brother (sister) eternal life.

"You promised paradise to the thief who repented; bring our brother (sister) to the joy of heaven.

"Our brother (sister) was washed in Baptism and anointed with the Holy Spirit; give *him* fellowship with all your saints.

"He was nourished with your Body and Blood; grant *him* a place at the table in your heavenly kingdom." (BCP 497)

If the eucharist is celebrated the service continues with the peace and the offertory. The meaning of this communion is well expressed in the proper postcommunion prayer:

"Grant that this Sacrament may be to us a comfort in affliction and a pledge of our inheritance in that kingdom where there is no death, neither sorrow nor crying, but the fullness of joy with all your saints." (BCP 498)

The service in the church concludes with The Commendation, an anthem and a prayer said over the body. A great Russian anthem for the departed from which we quoted earlier is given in the prayer book. (BCP 482, 499) It begins, "Give rest, O Christ, to your servant with your saints." The commendatory prayer expresses the prayer of the Church for the departed Christian that Christ will "receive *him* into the arms of his mercy, into the blessed rest of everlasting peace, and into the glorious company of the saints in light." (BCP 499)

Following the service in the church, the body is laid to rest. It may be cremated, buried in the earth or at sea. It is done "in sure and certain hope of the resurrection to eternal life through our Lord Jesus Christ" (BCP 501) and with prayer, "May *his* soul, and the souls of all the departed, through the mercy of God, rest in peace." (BCP 502)

The prayer book expresses the conflicting feelings with which Christians bury the dead in a final note at the end of the services:

"The very love we have for each other in Christ brings deep sorrow when we are parted by death. Jesus himself wept at the grave of his friend. So, while we rejoice that one we love has entered into the nearer presence of our Lord, we sorrow in sympathy with those who mourn." (BCP 507)

7
The Church at Worship

What does the prayer book tell us about worship?

The prayer book gives a formal answer to the question, "What is corporate worship?" in the catechism, An Outline of the Faith. That answer is,

> "In corporate worship, we unite ourselves with others to acknowledge the holiness of God, to hear God's Word, to offer prayer, and to celebrate the sacraments." (BCP 857)

This definition is little more than a summary of what we have found by looking at the actual services of The Book of Common Prayer. There we see worship presented as the common activity of the people of God assembled in his name and presence. The actual word *worship* means the acknowledgment of the worth of the one to whom the activity is directed and it is therefore an acknowledgment of the holiness and all the other attributes of God. Certainly for us as Christians the hearing of the word and the celebration of the sacraments are the chief activities that constitute worship and we see these expressed in the services of The Book of Common Prayer.

Worship, then, is an activity directed toward God, not toward the congregation. It is action in response to and called forth by God's saving activity directed toward us, and it is action to which we believe God in turn responds. Its purpose is to accept and enter into a relationship with God and, through God, with one another. That relationship is union through the person of Jesus Christ. He is the word of God. He is the resurrection and the life, a life we receive through sacramental worship. We offer ourselves to God in worship as he reveals himself to us in word and sacrament. He returns our lives to us renewed and made vehicles of the divine life just as he takes the bread and wine and returns them as communion in Christ's body and blood. In Eucharistic Prayer D, an ecumenical prayer based on a fourth century model, we pray,

> ". . . offering to you, *from the gifts you have given us*, this bread and this cup, we praise you and we bless you." (BCP 374, italics from author.)

We offer to God *from* the gifts he has given to us and God sends the Holy Spirit upon us and upon the gifts,

> ". . . sanctifying them and showing them to be holy gifts for your holy people, the bread of life and the cup of salvation, the Body and Blood of your Son Jesus Christ." (BCP 375)

God invites us to worship. God provides the gifts. We ourselves have nothing to offer. He accepts our offerings through Jesus Christ, our great high priest, and he returns them to us graced with his richest blessings, beyond our wildest imagining. The God who gave a son to redeem a slave (BCP 287) unites us to himself in the sacraments of Christ's dying and rising again and proclaims to us again and again in his holy word the good news of what he has done.

This activity is central to the life of the church and to the lives of the individual Christians. We literally cannot live without it. It *makes* us the people of God. It gives us the new life in Christ and the Holy Spirit.

What does the prayer book tell us about the church?

The prayer book, in its general introduction called Concerning the Service of the Church (BCP 13f) and in the specific arrangements it makes for particular services, exhibits the structure of the Church. It is a Church in which different orders fulfill different functions. "In all services," we read, "the entire Christian assembly participates in such a way that the members of each order within the Church, lay persons, bishops, priests, and deacons, fulfill the functions proper to their respective orders." (BCP 13)

The picture it paints is of the assembled Church presided over by its bishop, surrounded by a group of presbyters and assisted by deacons and lay persons (BCP 354) all acting in harmony to offer prayer and praise to God. It is an assembly which shows forth the love of Christ to the world by its inner love but knows that it does not live up to its own image. These are the questions which follow the affirmation of the Apostles' Creed in the baptismal service. They form a part of the baptismal covenant which all renew at confirmation, at the Great Vigil of Easter, and whenever they participate in a baptism.

"Will you continue in the apostles' teaching and fellowship, in the breaking of bread, and in the prayers?

"Will you persevere in resisting evil, and whenever you fall into sin, repent and return to the Lord?

"Will you proclaim by word and example the Good News of God in Christ?

"Will you seek and serve Christ in all persons, loving your neighbor as yourself?

"Will you strive for justice and peace among all people, and respect the dignity of every human being?" (BCP 304f)

The goals are clearly set forth: to continue in the apostolic faith and life, in prayer and eucharist, in mission and service to humanity, combating evil and seeking peace and justice. It is equally clear that failure, repentance and return are part of the picture. The great prayer of William Laud, the seventeenth-century Archbishop of Canterbury who died for his faith, expresses our Church's understanding of itself in vision and in reality:

"Gracious Father, we pray for thy holy Catholic Church. Fill it with all truth, in all truth with all peace. Where it is corrupt, purify it; where it is in error, direct it; where in anything it is amiss, reform it. Where it is right, strengthen it; where it is in want, provide for it; where it is divided, reunite it; for the sake of Jesus Christ thy Son our Savior." (BCP 816)

The church is a sacramental sign. It is the sign of Christ's presence and ministry in this world. But it is a sign composed of fallible and ignorant human beings who are always falling short of manifesting what Christ has declared them to be, the members of his body, one with the saints in glory, partakers of the resurrection, caught up into the life of God. As the bread, the sacramental sign of the body of Christ, still becomes soggy or mouldy, so we who are also a sacramental sign of the body of Christ are sinful and stupid. But that is only the sign. Christ remains himself.

How can we share this with others?

At the end of Daily Morning Prayer are three alternative collects for mission. The third asks,

> "Lord Jesus Christ, you stretched out your arms of love on the hard wood of the cross so that everyone might come within the reach of your saving embrace: So clothe us in your Spirit that we, reaching forth our hands in love, may bring those who do not know you to the knowledge and love of you; for the honor of your Name." (BCP 101)

The spirit of this prayer is repeated many times in The Book of Common Prayer. God does not shower his gifts upon us so that we can hoard them but so we can share them with others. The Church is a missionary society. We are always in danger, however, of preaching ourselves and not Christ Jesus as Lord. (cf. 2 Corinthians 4:5) We are in danger of trying to sell the Episcopal Church instead of bring people to Jesus. There is a difference!

The liturgy is the worship of God. It is not a means by which to accomplish something else. It is itself an end. It is the activity of the people of God, celebrating and renewing their relationship with him. Evangelism is reaching out to bring others into that relationship. The preaching of Jesus, the resurrection and the living of a new life in Christ in the midst of a hostile and disbelieving world, was the means by which the apostles brought others into their fellowship. The eucharist is the chief act of worship of the believing community on the Lord's day. It is not necessarily the best means of evangelism. It is, in fact, expecting a great deal of the Sunday eucharist not only to do the many things which we have seen that it does but also to attract converts and provide their instruction and spiritual formation.

The liturgy does, of course, attract converts. Russia is said to have accepted Eastern Orthodox Christianity in preference to Islam or to Western Catholicism because of the splendor and beauty of the liturgy its ambassadors witnessed at the church of Hagia Sophia in Constantinople. Many people are certainly attracted to the Episcopal Church by its liturgy. If the liturgy is the door by which people enter the Episcopal Church we need to provide them with other structures within the life of the parish to incorporate them into the life of the worshipping community. We have already mentioned the catechumenate as one such structure. It maintains its liturgical focus but includes moral and ethical instruction, formation in the life of prayer and participation in the church's social concerns. It also gives the newcomer the encouragement and support of a caring community. It is probably by being manifestly such a community and by reaching out into the wider community within which it is located rather than through powerful preaching and splendid services that the church can be most successful in drawing others into its life of worship and mission. Conversely the church which is not a community which shows forth the Christ-life will probably not attract many new members, no matter how splendid its liturgy.

One thing is certain. The treasures of The Book of Common Prayer and the joy of the worship of God in Christ have not been given to us to keep secret for our private enjoyment but to share with the world for which Christ died and rose again. At the end of the eucharist the Church does not encourage the faithful to remain in the sanctuary and bask in the warm glow of their communion with Christ. It sends them forth into the world "to love and serve the Lord." (BCP 366) In the Latin liturgy of the middle ages, this dismissal was, "*Ite, missa est.*" *Missa* is the Latin word for *sent*. It is the word from which *mission* is derived. It also became the most common Latin name for the eucharist, *missa*, the Mass. It is the central act of Christian worship itself, sending us forth as missionaries to bring the good news to our neighbors and to all humankind.

For further reading:

If you are interested in reading more about The Book of Common Prayer the following should be helpful:

Charles P. Price and Louis Weil, *Liturgy for Living*, The Church's Teaching Series, Harper & Row, San Francisco, 1979.

Marion J. Hatchett, *Commentary on the American Prayer Book*, Harper & Row, San Francisco, 1980.

Liturgy for Living contains a glossary of liturgical terms and an extensive bibliography for further reading.

Leonel L. Mitchell, *Praying Shapes Believing, a theological commentary of* The Book of Common Prayer, Morehouse, Harrisburg, 1991.

The Book of Occasional Services [BOS] and *Lesser Feasts and Fasts* [LFF] are official publications of the Episcopal Church approved by the General Convention. They are published by the Church Hymnal Corporation, 800 Second Avenue, New York, NY 10017.

From Forward Movement Publications:

Holy Communion for Children

The Book of Common Prayer in the Life of the Episcopal Church

The Eucharist with Notes

The Prayers of the People: ways to make them your own

What Is Liturgy?